*this
self-care journal
belongs to:*

_____

dated:

_____

this edition of love yours is a tool to ensure that you are putting yourself first. write down your affirmations, see your words take shape and document your growth.

XO,
ASH
&
CORT

january 1

JANUARY AFFIRIMATIONS.

_____

_____

_____

_____

_____

_____

_____

_____

to love is to be loved.

january 2

OFTEN TIMES WE FIND OURSELVES FEELING INADEQUATE. ASSURE YOURSELF RIGHT NOW THAT YOU ARE ENOUGH.

_____

_____

_____

_____

_____

_____

_____

_____

january 3

REMIND YOURSELF ON HOW AND WHY YOU ARE NEVER ALONE.

_____

_____

_____

_____

_____

_____

_____

_____

january 4

WHAT DO YOU HAVE A PASSION FOR?

_____

_____

_____

_____

_____

_____

_____

_____

_____

january 5

WHAT ARE YOUR INSECURITIES AND HOW ARE YOU OVERCOMING THEM?

_____
_____
_____
_____
_____
_____
_____
_____

january 6

BUILD YOURSELF UP.

january 7

NAME THE WAYS THAT YOU FIND YOUR HAPPY PLACE.

_____

_____

_____

_____

_____

_____

_____

_____

january 8

HOW DO YOU EMBRACE CHANGE?

january 9

I NO LONGER FEED MY ENERGY TO _____

_____

_____

_____

_____

_____

_____

_____

_____

january 10

WHAT WAYS CAN YOU BE MORE OUTGOING?

january 11

IF YOU COULD CHANGE ANYTHING ABOUT THE WORLD, WHAT WOULD IT BE?

january 12

DO YOU HAVE ANY BATTLES WITH YOUR EGO? IF SO, IN WHAT WAYS?

january 13

WHAT ARE YOU COMMITTED TO ACCEPTING ABOUT YOURSELF?

_____
_____
_____
_____
_____
_____
_____
_____
_____

january 14

WHAT IS A CHILDHOOD MEMORY THAT MAKES YOU SMILE?

_____

_____

_____

_____

_____

_____

_____

_____

january 15

WHAT GOOD DEEDS HAVE YOU DONE THIS MONTH?

_____

_____

_____

_____

_____

_____

_____

_____

january 16

WRITE DOWN YOUR BUCKET LIST TRAVEL DESTINATIONS.

january 17

WHAT'S THE RELATIONSHIP THAT YOU HAVE WITH YOUR BODY?

_____
_____
_____
_____
_____
_____
_____
_____
_____

january 18

WHO'S YOUR FAVORITE PERSON AND WHY?

january 19

HOW ARE YOU FEELING TODAY?

_____

_____

_____

_____

_____

_____

_____

_____

_____

january 20

WHEN DO YOU TRUST YOURSELF THE MOST?

january 21

NAME A SINGLE EVENT THAT CHANGED YOUR LIFE FOR THE BETTER.

_____
_____
_____
_____
_____
_____
_____
_____

january 22

I FORGIVE MY BODY FOR _____.

_____
_____
_____
_____
_____
_____
_____
_____
_____

january 23

HOW ARE YOU TRIGGERED BY THE NEWS THAT YOU READ/SEE?

_____

_____

_____

_____

_____

_____

_____

_____

january 24

IN WHAT WAYS HAVE YOU BEEN PROACTIVE?

january 25

VENT HERE.

_____

_____

_____

_____

_____

_____

_____

_____

january 26

HOW ARE YOU BECOMING MORE FINANCIALLY RESPONSIBLE?

january 27

WRITE A LOVE LETTER TO YOURSELF.

january 28

WHAT WAS THE LAST SITUATION THAT FORCED YOU TO TALK TO SOMEONE?

_____
_____
_____
_____
_____
_____
_____
_____

january 29

SHOW YOURSELF GRATITUDE.

_____

_____

_____

_____

_____

_____

_____

_____

_____

january 30

TODAY I AM THANKFUL FOR...

january 31

TIME TO REFLECT ON THIS MONTH.
(FEELINGS, ACCOMPLISHMENTS, ETC.)

_____

_____

_____

_____

_____

_____

_____

_____

february 1

FEBRUARY AFFIRMATIONS.

_____

_____

_____

_____

_____

_____

_____

_____

_____

february 2

WHEN DO YOU FEEL THE HAPPIEST?

_____

_____

_____

_____

_____

_____

_____

_____

february 3

WHEN WAS THE LAST TIME YOU GOT DRESSED UP AND WHERE DID YOU GO?

february 4

WHAT IS THE NEXT LEVEL YOU ARE STRIVING FOR IN LIFE?

___
___
___
___
___
___
___
___

february 5

WHAT DO YOU LOVE MOST ABOUT YOURSELF AND WHY?

_____

_____

_____

_____

_____

_____

_____

_____

february 6

WHAT ARE SOME THINGS THAT TEST YOUR PATIENCE?

---

february 7

IN WHAT WAYS DO YOU OVERLOOK YOURSELF?

february 8

HOW ARE YOU INVESTING IN YOURSELF?

_____

_____

_____

_____

_____

_____

_____

_____

february 9

WHO'S CURRENTLY MAKING YOU HAPPY AND HOW?

february 10

NAME THREE SMALL GOALS FOR THE MONTH.

_____

_____

_____

_____

_____

_____

_____

february 11

WHAT ARE YOUR PERSONAL TRAITS THAT MAKE YOU FEEL SPECIAL?

_____

_____

_____

_____

_____

_____

_____

_____

february 12

WHAT ADVICE HAVE YOU HELD ON TO THAT'S HELPED YOU IN LIFE?

_____

_____

_____

_____

_____

_____

_____

_____

february 13

IN WHAT WAYS ARE YOU CELEBRATING YOURSELF?

_____
_____
_____
_____
_____
_____
_____
_____
_____

february 14

WHEN WAS THE LAST TIME YOU HAD A GOOD CRY?

february 15

WHAT DO YOU FORGIVE YOURSELF FOR?

_____
_____
_____
_____
_____
_____
_____
_____
_____

february 16

WHAT ARE YOUR FAVORITE THINGS TO DO WITH YOUR ME TIME?

_____

_____

_____

_____

_____

_____

_____

february 17

WHO OR WHAT DISAPPOINTED YOU LATELY AND HOW ARE YOU DEALING WITH IT?

_____

_____

_____

_____

_____

_____

_____

_____

february 18

IT HURTS MY FEELINGS WHEN

_____

_____

_____

_____

_____

_____

_____

february 19

ANY ROOM FOR NEW FRIENDS? WHY OR WHY NOT?

_____
_____
_____
_____
_____
_____
_____
_____

february 20

BIGGEST REGRET? WRITE IT DOWN, RELEASE AND LET GO.

_____

_____

_____

_____

_____

_____

_____

february 21

I'M NO LONGER UPSET ABOUT

_____

_____

_____

_____

_____

_____

_____

_____

_____

replinish yourself first.

february 22

IN WHAT WAYS ARE YOU BEING KIND TO YOUR BODY?

february 23

CONFRONT YOUR TRIGGERS.

february 24

HOW MUCH ATTENTION HAVE YOU GIVEN YOURSELF LATELY?

_____

_____

_____

_____

_____

_____

_____

_____

_____

february 25

HOW HAS TRAUMA AFFECTED YOUR LIFE?

_____

_____

_____

_____

_____

_____

_____

_____

february 26

I APPRECIATE MYSELF FOR

_____

_____

_____

_____

_____

_____

_____

_____

february 27

LIST THE SMALL VICTORIES THAT YOU ARE CURRENTLY CELEBRATING.

_____
_____
_____
_____
_____
_____
_____
_____

february 28

HOW HAVE YOU EMPOWERED YOURSELF TO PUSH FORWARD LATELY?

_____
_____
_____
_____
_____
_____
_____
_____

february 29

TIME TO REFLECT ON THIS MONTH.
(FEELINGS, ACCOMPLISHMENTS, ETC.)

_____

_____

_____

_____

_____

_____

_____

_____

march 1

MARCH AFFIRMATION.

_____

_____

_____

_____

_____

_____

_____

_____

_____

march 2

HOW DO THE PEOPLE AROUND YOU ADD VALUE TO YOUR LIFE?

_____

_____

_____

_____

_____

_____

_____

_____

march 3

HOW MUCH DO YOU TRUST YOURSELF?

_____

_____

_____

_____

_____

_____

_____

_____

_____

march 4

WHAT WOULD YOU SAY ARE SOME OF YOUR PERSONAL GIFTS?

march 5

HOW DO YOU ACCEPT YOUR NEGATIVE QUALITIES?

march 6

HOW CAN YOU MAKE TIME TO DO THE THINGS THAT YOU ENJOY?

___
___
___
___
___
___
___

march 7

PRIDE DOES NOT ALLOW ME TO .....

_____
_____
_____
_____
_____
_____
_____
_____

march 8

REFLECT ON THE THINGS THAT YOU ARE GRATEFUL FOR.

_____

_____

_____

_____

_____

_____

_____

march 9

WHAT ARE SOME CHARACTERISTICS THAT PEOPLE WOULD SAY YOU POSSESS?

march 10

WHAT ARE YOU MOST SECURE ABOUT?

_____
_____
_____
_____
_____
_____
_____
_____

march 11

WHAT ARE SOME NEGATIVE PERCEPTIONS THAT YOU'VE HEARD ABOUT YOURSELF?

_____
_____
_____
_____
_____
_____
_____
_____

march 12

WHO OR WHAT DISAPPOINTED YOU LATELY AND HOW ARE YOU DEALING WITH IT?

march 13

WHAT ARE SOME THINGS THAT YOU'VE OVERCOME THAT YOU'RE PROUD OF?

_____

_____

_____

_____

_____

_____

_____

_____

march 14

HOW DO YOU CELEBRATE THE SMALL VICTORIES?

_____

_____

_____

_____

_____

_____

_____

march 15

I FEEL COMPLETE BECAUSE...

_____
_____
_____
_____
_____
_____
_____
_____
_____

march 16

FOLLOW YOUR FIRST MIND. WHAT ARE YOU SECOND GUESSING AT THE MOMENT?

march 17

HOW HAVE THINGS BEEN WORKING IN YOUR FAVOR LATELY?

_____
_____
_____
_____
_____
_____
_____
_____

march 18

IN WHAT WAYS ARE YOU OVER EXERTING YOURSELF?

_____

_____

_____

_____

_____

_____

_____

march 19

WHAT HAVE YOU FORGIVEN YOURSELF FOR?

_____

_____

_____

_____

_____

_____

_____

_____

_____

march 20

WHERE DOES YOUR INSPIRATION COME FROM?

_____
_____
_____
_____
_____
_____
_____
_____

WHAT EXPECTATIONS HAVE YOU SET FOR YOURSELF THAT YOU FIND UNNECESSARY?

_____
_____
_____
_____
_____
_____
_____
_____

march 22

WHAT DOES UNCONDITIONAL LOVE MEAN TO YOU?

_____

_____

_____

_____

_____

_____

_____

march 23

DESCRIBE YOURSELF IN 10 WORDS.

WHAT IS YOUR BODY SAYING TO YOU RIGHT NOW?

_____
_____
_____
_____
_____
_____
_____
_____

WHAT ARE YOUR BEST INNER QUALITIES?

_____

_____

_____

_____

_____

_____

_____

_____

_____

march 26

WHAT DO YOU FIND YOURSELF DOING IN YOUR FREE TIME?

_____
_____
_____
_____
_____
_____
_____
_____

march 27

WHAT IS THE BRAVEST THING YOU'VE EVER DONE?

_____

_____

_____

_____

_____

_____

_____

_____

march 28

WHAT ARE SOME OF YOUR WEAKNESSES?

_____

_____

_____

_____

_____

_____

_____

_____

WHEN WAS THE LAST TIME YOU FELT ANXIOUS AND WHY?

_____

_____

_____

_____

_____

_____

_____

_____

march 30

WHO ARE YOU AND WHAT DO YOU REPRESENT?

_____

_____

_____

_____

_____

_____

_____

_____

TIME TO REFLECT ON THIS MONTH.
(FEELINGS, ACCOMPLISHMENTS, ETC.)

_____

_____

_____

_____

_____

_____

_____

_____

let that sh*t go.

april 1

APRIL AFFIRMATIONS.

_____

_____

_____

_____

_____

_____

_____

_____

_____

april 2

HOW DO YOU NEGLECT YOUR BODY?

_____

_____

_____

_____

_____

_____

_____

_____

april 3

HOW DOES YOUR MIND REMIND YOU THAT IT'S TIME TO TAKE A BREAK?

_____

_____

_____

_____

_____

_____

_____

_____

april 4

WHAT DOES A PERFECT DAY LOOK LIKE FOR YOU?

_____

_____

_____

_____

_____

_____

_____

april 5

WHAT IS TIME REVEALING ABOUT YOUR CHILDHOOD?

_____

_____

_____

_____

_____

_____

_____

_____

april 6

WHAT ARE YOUR BEST RELATIONSHIP QUALITIES?

_____

_____

_____

_____

_____

_____

_____

_____

april 7

WHEN HAVE YOU PUSHED YOURSELF BEYOND YOUR COMFORT ZONE?

_____

_____

_____

_____

_____

_____

_____

_____

april 8

HOW DO YOU SHOW YOUR UNCONDITIONAL LOVE TO THOSE CLOSES TO YOU?

april 9

HOW ARE YOU CURRENTLY IMPACTING OTHERS?

_____

_____

_____

_____

_____

_____

_____

_____

april 10

NAME SOMETHING YOU'VE DONE TODAY THAT MADE YOU HAPPY.

april 11

IN WHAT WAYS DO YOU TEND TO HINDER YOURSELF FROM THRIVING?

april 12

THE LEFT SIDE OF THE BRAIN HAS TO DO WITH LOGIC. HOW HAVE YOU BEEN EXERCISING THE LEFT SIDE OF YOUR BRAIN?

april 13

HOW HAVE YOU BEEN STAYING ON BUDGET THIS MONTH?

_____

_____

_____

_____

_____

_____

_____

_____

april 14

HOW ARE YOUR ANXIETY LEVELS? EXPLAIN

april 15

WRITE A LETTER TO YOUR FUTURE SELF.

_____

_____

_____

_____

_____

_____

_____

_____

_____

april 16

WHAT ARE YOUR RECENT DREAMS TELLING YOU ABOUT YOURSELF?

_____
_____
_____
_____
_____
_____
_____
_____

april 17

IN WHAT WAYS ARE YOU MISUNDERSTOOD?

_____

_____

_____

_____

_____

_____

_____

_____

_____

april 18

WHAT IS YOUR BIGGEST FEAR? WRITE IT DOWN, RELEASE AND LET GO.

_____
_____
_____
_____
_____
_____
_____

april 19

I AM A SURVIVOR BECAUSE .....

_____

_____

_____

_____

_____

_____

_____

_____

april 20

THE MIRROR CAN BE A SCARY PLACE FOR THOSE WHO REFUSE TO FACE THEMSELVES. HOW ARE YOU HOLDING YOURSELF ACCOUNTABLE?

_____
_____
_____
_____
_____
_____
_____
_____

april 21

HOW HAS TRAUMA AFFECTED YOUR LIFE?

_____

_____

_____

_____

_____

_____

_____

_____

_____

april 22

WHAT ARE HEALTHY WAYS THAT YOU DEAL WITH STRESSFUL TIMES?

_____

_____

_____

_____

_____

_____

_____

april 23

IN WHAT WAYS CAN YOU BE TOO CRITICAL OF YOURSELF?

_____

_____

_____

_____

_____

_____

_____

_____

_____

april 24

PEOPLE TEND TO GIVE THE BEST ADVICE TO OTHERS, WHAT IS SOME GOOD ADVICE YOU CAN GIVE TO YOURSELF?

_____
_____
_____
_____
_____
_____
_____

april 25

TIME IS A VALUABLE THING TO WASTE, WHAT ARE YOU NO LONGER INVESTING TIME IN?

_____

_____

_____

_____

_____

_____

_____

_____

april 26

WRITE A LETTER TO THE PERSON THAT LET YOU DOWN THE MOST. RELEASE IT AND LET IT GO.

_____
_____
_____
_____
_____
_____
_____
_____

april 27

HOW DID YOU LOVE ON YOURSELF TODAY?

_____

_____

_____

_____

_____

_____

_____

_____

april 28

WHO SHOULD YOU CUT OUT OF YOUR LIFE AND WHY?

april 29

WHAT IS YOUR PURPOSE IN LIFE?

_____

_____

_____

_____

_____

_____

_____

_____

_____

april 30

TIME TO REFLECT ON THIS MONTH. (FEELINGS, ACCOMPLISHMENTS, ETC.)

_____

_____

_____

_____

_____

_____

_____

_____

may 1

MAY AFFIRMATIONS.

_____

_____

_____

_____

_____

_____

_____

_____

_____

may 2

IN WHAT WAYS ARE YOU BEING KIND TO YOUR BODY?

_____
_____
_____
_____
_____
_____
_____
_____

may 3

WHO OWES YOU AN APOLOGY AND WHY?

_____

_____

_____

_____

_____

_____

_____

_____

may 4

WHAT ARE YOU CURRENTLY INTERESTED IN.

_____

_____

_____

_____

_____

_____

_____

_____

may 5

EVEN IF IT'S NOT NEEDED AT THE MOMENT, HAVE A 1 ON 1 WITH YOURSELF NOW.

may 6

NOW IS THE PERFECT TIME TO TAKE CONTROL OF YOUR THOUGHTS. WRITE THEM FREELY AND CONTROL YOUR NARRATIVE.

_____

_____

_____

_____

_____

_____

_____

_____

may 7

LIST THE THINGS THAT EXIST IN YOUR UTOPIA.

_____

_____

_____

_____

_____

_____

_____

_____

may 8

COMPLIMENT YOURSELF.

_____

_____

_____

_____

_____

_____

_____

_____

_____

may 9

WHAT IS SOMETHING YOU WOULD LIKE TO WORK ON/CREATE THAT HASN'T BEEN PURSUED?

may 10

BREAK THE HABIT OF PESSIMISM. HOW ARE YOU BEING OPTIMISTIC ABOUT YOUR FUTURE?

_____
_____
_____
_____
_____
_____
_____

may 11

WHAT WEAKNESSES HAVE YOU TURNED INTO STRENGTHS?

_____

_____

_____

_____

_____

_____

_____

_____

may 12

IT HURTS MY FEELINGS WHEN......

_____

_____

_____

_____

_____

_____

_____

_____

_____

may 13

HOW ARE YOU STAYING EMOTIONALLY BALANCED?

_____

_____

_____

_____

_____

_____

_____

_____

what's meant for you, is already yours.

may 14

I HAVE THE POWER TO......

_____
_____
_____
_____
_____
_____
_____
_____
_____

may 15

WHAT ARE SOME THINGS THAT YOU RECENTLY LEARNED ABOUT YOURSELF?

_____

_____

_____

_____

_____

_____

_____

may 16

WHAT THINGS DO YOU FEEL PRESSURED TO ENGAGE IN SOCIALLY THAT YOU DON'T CARE FOR?

may 17

WHAT MATTERS THE MOST IN YOUR LIFE RIGHT NOW?

may 18

HOW ARE YOU A BETTER PERSON THAN YOU WERE 5 YEARS AGO?

_____

_____

_____

_____

_____

_____

_____

may 19

IN WHAT WAYS DO YOU MAKE YOURSELF EASY TO LOVE?

_____

_____

_____

_____

_____

_____

_____

_____

may 20

I HAVE FAITH THAT.....

_____

_____

_____

_____

_____

_____

_____

_____

may 21

HOW ARE YOU BEING TAKEN ADVANTAGE OF?

may 22

WHAT WORRIES YOU ABOUT YOUR FUTURE? RELEASE THAT ENERGY OF WORRYING.

_____

_____

_____

_____

_____

_____

_____

may 23

PLAN AN ENTIRE SELF CARE OFF DAY.

_____

_____

_____

_____

_____

_____

_____

_____

may 24

HOW DO YOU FEEL ABOUT SEEING A PERSONAL LIFE COACH OR THERAPIST?

_____
_____
_____
_____
_____
_____
_____
_____

may 25

WHAT IS SOMETHING YOU CAN ADD TO YOUR DAY TO DAY ROUTINE THAT'LL BRING YOU JOY?

_____

_____

_____

_____

_____

_____

_____

_____

may 26

NAME 3 THINGS THAT OTHER PEOPLE APPRECIATE ABOUT YOU.

_____

_____

_____

_____

_____

_____

_____

_____

_____

may 27

WHAT ARE SOME OF YOUR TRIGGERS?

may 28

WHEN WAS THE LAST TIME YOU MADE ASSUMPTIONS AND WHY?

_____

_____

_____

_____

_____

_____

_____

_____

may 29

WOULD YOU RATHER FAIL OR NEVER TRY? WHY?

_____
_____
_____
_____
_____
_____
_____
_____
_____

may 30

WHAT HOLDS SENTIMENTAL VALUE TO YOU?

_____

_____

_____

_____

_____

_____

_____

_____

_____

may 31

TIME TO REFLECT ON THIS MONTH. (FEELINGS, ACCOMPLISHMENTS, ETC.)

_____

_____

_____

_____

_____

_____

_____

_____

june 1

JUNE AFFIRMATIONS.

_____

_____

_____

_____

_____

_____

_____

_____

_____

june 2

HOW ARE YOU MANAGING YOUR FREE TIME?

_____

_____

_____

_____

_____

_____

_____

_____

june 3

HOW DO YOU SEE YOURSELF?

_____

_____

_____

_____

_____

_____

_____

_____

_____

june 4

IF YOU COULD START A NONPROFIT, WHAT WOULD BE THE PURPOSE BEHIND IT?

june 5

WHEN YOU SCROLL YOUR TIMELINE WHAT DO YOU SEE AND HOW DOES IT MAKE YOU FEEL?

_____

_____

_____

_____

_____

_____

_____

june 6

WHAT WAS THE TOUGHEST THING YOU EVER HAD TO DO?

_____
_____
_____
_____
_____
_____
_____

june 7

WHERE DO YOU HAVE TO BE IN LIFE TO FILL COMPLETELY FULFILLED?

_____

_____

_____

_____

_____

_____

_____

_____

june 8

WHAT'S SOMETHING YOU ONCE GAVE UP ON THAT YOU'VE PICKED BACK UP?

_____
_____
_____
_____
_____
_____
_____

TAKE THESE 3 WORDS AND WRITE THE FIRST THOUGHT THAT COMES TO MIND: STRONG, VUNERABLE, PASSION.

THE RIGHT SIDE OF THE BRAIN IS WHERE CREATIVITY IS BORN. HOW HAVE YOU BEEN ACTIVATING THE RIGHT SIDE OF YOUR BRAIN?

_____

_____

_____

_____

_____

_____

_____

_____

june 11

HOW HAS LIFE BEEN TREATING YOU?

_____

_____

_____

_____

_____

_____

_____

_____

june 12

WHAT'S YOUR FAVORITE SEASON AND WHY?

_____

_____

_____

_____

_____

_____

_____

_____

june 13

IN WHAT WAYS ARE YOU WISER?

_____
_____
_____
_____
_____
_____
_____
_____

june 14

WHAT IS SOMETHING YOU DID THAT YOU'RE NOT PROUD OF. (WRITE IT DOWN, FORGIVE YOURSELF AND LET IT GO)

_____

_____

_____

_____

_____

_____

_____

_____

_____

june 15

HOW DO YOU PRACTICE INTIMACY WITH YOURSELF?

_____

_____

_____

_____

_____

_____

_____

_____

june 16

WHEN WAS THE LAST TIME YOU SAID I LOVE YOU AND WHY?

_____

_____

_____

_____

_____

_____

_____

june 17

WHAT DO YOU LOVE THE MOST ABOUT YOURSELF?

_____

_____

_____

_____

_____

_____

_____

_____

june 18

WHAT DOES YOUR TRUTH FEEL LIKE?

_____
_____
_____
_____
_____
_____
_____
_____

june 19

WHAT TYPE OF PERSON WOULD YOUR FAMILY DESCRIBE YOU AS?

_____

_____

_____

_____

_____

_____

_____

_____

june 20

WHAT IS SOMETHING THAT HAS BECOME REDUNDANT TO YOU?

_____
_____
_____
_____
_____
_____
_____
_____

june 21

WHAT GOT THE BEST OF YOU BEFORE THAT YOU HANDLE DIFFERENTLY NOW?

_____
_____
_____
_____
_____
_____
_____
_____

june 22

WHAT IS SOMETHING VERY FEW KNOW ABOUT YOU?

_____
_____
_____
_____
_____
_____
_____
_____

june 23

WHAT ARE 3 WAYS IN WHICH YOU AFFIRM YOURSELF EVERYDAY?

_____
_____
_____
_____
_____
_____
_____
_____

june 24

WHAT IS SOME MEANINGFUL ADVICE YOU RECENTLY RECEIVED?

_____

_____

_____

_____

_____

_____

_____

_____

june 25

WHAT IS THE MOST IMPORTANT THING THAT YOU ARE DOING WITH YOUR LIFE?

_____

_____

_____

_____

_____

_____

_____

june 26

HOW ARE YOU PUTTING THE NEEDS OF OTHERS BEFORE YOUR OWN?

june 27

WHAT SITUATION ARE YOU CURRENTLY EMPATHETIC TOWARDS?

_____

_____

_____

_____

_____

_____

_____

_____

june 28

PAINT THE PERFECT PICTURE ON HOW YOU NEED TO BE LOVED.

_____

_____

_____

_____

_____

_____

_____

_____

june 29

HOW ARE YOUR SLEEP PATTERNS AND HOW DO THEY AFFECT YOUR DAYS?

_____

_____

_____

_____

_____

_____

_____

_____

june 30

TIME TO REFLECT ON THIS MONTH. (FEELINGS, ACCOMPLISHMENTS, ETC.)

_____

_____

_____

_____

_____

_____

_____

_____

july 1

JULY AFFIRMATIONS.

_____

_____

_____

_____

_____

_____

_____

_____

_____

july 2

HOW DO YOU MAKE YOURSELF FEEL AT HOME WHEN YOU'RE IN AN UNFAMILIAR PLACE?

july 3

VENT HERE.

we measure ourselves through other people's perception. that does not add up.

july 4

WHAT'S A LESSON THAT HAS TAKEN TIME TO LEARN?

july 5

WHAT'S THE DIFFERENCE IN BEING ALONE AND BEING LONELY?

_____

_____

_____

_____

_____

_____

_____

july 6

NAME THE PEOPLE THAT GENUINELY SUPPORT YOU AND THANK THEM. TAKE THE TIME OUT TO TELL THEM THIS WEEK.

july 7

HOW ARE YOU POURING INTO YOURSELF?

_____

_____

_____

_____

_____

_____

_____

_____

_____

july 8

WHAT WAS THE MOST FREEING EXPERIENCE YOU'VE EVER HAD?

_____
_____
_____
_____
_____
_____
_____
_____

july 9

WHAT WAS THE BEST RELATIONSHIP YOU'VE HAD?

_____
_____
_____
_____
_____
_____
_____
_____

july 10

WHAT DO YOU BRING TO THE TABLE IN A RELATIONSHIP?

_____
_____
_____
_____
_____
_____
_____

july 11

WHAT HAVE YOU DOUBTED BEFORE THAT YOU WERE ABLE TO ACHIEVE? RELEASE THAT ENERGY OF SELF-DOUBT?

_____
_____
_____
_____
_____
_____
_____
_____

july 12

IF YOU ARE FEELING ALONE, HOW DO YOU REMIND YOURSELF THAT YOU ARE NOT?

_____

_____

_____

_____

_____

_____

_____

july 13

WHAT SMALL ACT OF KINDNESS HAVE YOU COMMITTED THIS WEEK?

_____
_____
_____
_____
_____
_____
_____
_____

july 14

WHAT ARE YOUR STANDARDS WHILE DATING?

_____

_____

_____

_____

_____

_____

_____

_____

july 15

ARE THERE ANY CYCLES THAT YOU'VE NOTICED YOURSELF IN? IF SO, WHAT ARE THEY AND WHAT ARE YOUR PLANS TO BREAK THEM?

_____

_____

_____

_____

_____

_____

_____

_____

july 16

WHAT LIES WERE YOU TOLD AS A CHILD THAT YOU'RE NOW DISCOVERING THE TRUTH ABOUT?

_____

_____

_____

_____

_____

_____

_____

_____

july 17

WHAT'S ONE POSITIVE THING THAT HAS HAPPENED TO OR AROUND YOU TODAY?

_____

_____

_____

_____

_____

_____

_____

_____

july 18

WRITE ABOUT A MOMENT THAT YOU HAD A FULL BODY EXPERIENCE. WHETHER IT WAS A LUCID DREAM OR SOMETHING THAT GAVE YOU CHILLS.

july 19

HOW ARE YOU SUPPORTING THOSE CLOSE TO YOU?

_____

_____

_____

_____

_____

_____

_____

_____

july 20

WHAT IS YOUR INTUITION TELLING YOU THAT YOU MAY BE IGNORING?

_____
_____
_____
_____
_____
_____
_____
_____
_____

july 21

WHAT WILL YOU BE REMEMBERED FOR?

_____

_____

_____

_____

_____

_____

_____

_____

july 22

HOW DO YOU FEEL ABOUT BEING ALONE?

_____
_____
_____
_____
_____
_____
_____
_____
_____

july 23

ARE YOU AWARE OF THE THINGS THAT DRAIN YOUR ENERGY? WHAT ARE THEY?

_____
_____
_____
_____
_____
_____
_____
_____

july 24

HOW DOES BEING OVER CRITICAL OF YOURSELF HINDER YOU?

_____
_____
_____
_____
_____
_____
_____
_____

july 25

HOW DO YOU GET CAUGHT UP IN PROBLEMS THAT ARE NOT YOUR OWN?

_____
_____
_____
_____
_____
_____
_____
_____

july 26

IN ORDER TO CONTROL YOUR MIND, YOU MUST LISTEN TO YOURSELF MORE. HOW ARE YOU CONTROLLING YOUR MIND?

_____
_____
_____
_____
_____
_____
_____
_____

july 27

EVERYONE HAS A DIFFERENT PERSPECTIVE OF SUCCESS, WHAT DOES SUCCESS LOOK LIKE FOR YOU?

july 28

WHAT ARE YOU NOT FOLLOWING THROUGH WITH?

_____

_____

_____

_____

_____

_____

_____

_____

_____

july 29

WHAT ARE SOME PIECES OF YOURSELF THAT YOU HAVE NOT QUITE HEALED?

_____
_____
_____
_____
_____
_____
_____
_____

july 30

HOW HAVE YOU ADDRESSED THINGS THAT HAVE BOTHERED YOU FROM THE PAST?

_____
_____
_____
_____
_____
_____
_____
_____
_____

july 31

TIME TO REFLECT ON THIS MONTH. (FEELINGS, ACCOMPLISHMENTS, ETC.)

_____

_____

_____

_____

_____

_____

_____

_____

august 1

AUGUST AFFIRMATIONS.

_____

_____

_____

_____

_____

_____

_____

_____

august 2

WHAT ARE YOU NO LONGER ACCEPTING FROM ANYONE?

_____
_____
_____
_____
_____
_____
_____
_____

august 3

WHAT ARE SOME SHORT-TERM GOALS THAT YOU'VE SET RECENTLY?

august 4

WHAT BOUNDARIES ARE YOU SETTING IN YOUR LIFE?

_____

_____

_____

_____

_____

_____

_____

_____

august 4

IF YOU COULD GIVE YOUR YOUNGER SELF ADVICE ABOUT LIFE. WHAT WOULD IT BE?

august 5

HOW HAVE YOU DIMMED YOUR LIGHT FOR OTHERS TO SHINE?

august 6

HOW DO YOU COPE WHEN YOUR DARKNESS SHOWS ITSELF?

august 7

august 8

NAME THREES WAYS IN WHICH A CHANGE OF MINDSET HAS CLEARED THE PATH FOR NEW BEGINNINGS.

_____

_____

_____

_____

_____

_____

_____

_____

august 9

IF IT WON'T MATTER IN 5 YEARS, WHY WORRY ABOUT IT NOW. WHAT ARE SOME WORRIES THAT YOU KNOW WON'T MATTER LATER IN LIFE?

august 10

WHAT ARE YOUR BELIEFS AND HOW DOES IT KEEP YOU GROUNDED?

_____

_____

_____

_____

_____

_____

_____

_____

august 11

RESEARCH YOUR LIFE PATH NUMBER AND WRITE DOWN HOW IT RESONATES WITH YOU.

_____
_____
_____
_____
_____
_____
_____
_____
_____

august 12

HOW DID YOU COPE WITH A BAD BREAK UP?

_____

_____

_____

_____

_____

_____

_____

_____

_____

august 13

IN WHAT WAYS DO YOU GIVE BACK TO OTHERS?

_____

_____

_____

_____

_____

_____

_____

august 14

WHAT HAVE YOU ALWAYS BEEN CURIOUS ABOUT?

_____

_____

_____

_____

_____

_____

_____

_____

august 15

WHERE DO YOU GET YOUR STRENGTH FROM?

_____

_____

_____

_____

_____

_____

_____

august 16

WHO DO YOU OWE AN APOLOGY TO AND WHY? (ACCOUNTABILITY QUESTION)

_____

_____

_____

_____

_____

_____

_____

_____

august 17

WHAT QUALITIES ABOUT YOURSELF THAT COULD POSSIBLY PUSH PEOPLE AWAY?

_____

_____

_____

_____

_____

_____

_____

_____

august 18

WHAT ARE YOU CURRENTLY MANIFESTING?

_____
_____
_____
_____
_____
_____
_____
_____

august 19

**WHAT WOULD BE YOUR DREAM VACATION?
(PLACE, VACATION LENGTH, TRAVEL BUDDY, ETC.)**

august 20

HOW DO YOU FIND TIME TO RELAX EVERYDAY?

august 21

HOW HAS SELF-LOVE MADE YOU A BETTER PERSON?

_____

_____

_____

_____

_____

_____

_____

_____

august 22

WHAT WAYS WOULD YOU LIKE TO BE MORE TRANSPARENT?

_____

_____

_____

_____

_____

_____

_____

_____

_____

august 23

HOW DO YOU WANT TO BE ROMANTICALLY LOVED?

_____

_____

_____

_____

_____

_____

_____

_____

_____

august 24

WHAT MAKES YOU FEEL THE MOST LIBERATED?

_____

_____

_____

_____

_____

_____

_____

_____

august 25

WRITE DOWN ANYTHING THAT'S CURRENTLY STRESSING YOU. RELEASE AND LET IT GO.

_____

_____

_____

_____

_____

_____

_____

_____

august 26

IS THERE ANYONE YOU'RE HOLDING ON TO THAT YOU SHOULDN'T? WHY OR WHY NOT?

_____

_____

_____

_____

_____

_____

_____

_____

august 27

IN WHAT WAYS HAVE YOU BEEN A GOOD FRIEND?

_____
_____
_____
_____
_____
_____
_____
_____

simply planning out the next phase in life can alleviate unwanted stress.

august 28

WHO'S CURRENTLY MAKING YOU HAPPY AND HOW?

_____

_____

_____

_____

_____

_____

_____

_____

august 29

WE HOLD ON TO BAGGAGE THAT IS NOT OUR OWN. HOW ARE LETTING GO OF INHERITED TRAUMA?

_____

_____

_____

_____

_____

_____

_____

_____

august 30

LIST THE WAYS IN WHICH YOUR HEALING PROCESS HAS BEGAN.

_____

_____

_____

_____

_____

_____

_____

_____

august 31

TIME TO REFLECT ON THIS MONTH. (FEELINGS, ACCOMPLISHMENTS, ETC.)

_____
_____
_____
_____
_____
_____
_____
_____
_____

september 1

SEPTEMBER AFFIRMATIONS.

_____

_____

_____

_____

_____

_____

_____

_____

_____

september 2

NAME A TIME WHEN YOU WERE ABLE TO LEARN FROM AN EXPERIENCE THAT COULD HAVE BROKEN YOU.

_____
_____
_____
_____
_____
_____
_____
_____
_____

september 3

CHANGE STARTS IN THE MIND. WHAT ARE YOU UNLEARNING AND RELEARNING?

september 4

IN WHAT WAYS ARE YOU CELEBRATING YOURSELF?

_____
_____
_____
_____
_____
_____
_____
_____
_____

september 5

IT'S OK TO SAY NO. WHAT/WHO HAVE YOU SAID NO TO LATELY AND HOW DID IT MAKE YOU FEEL?

september 6

VENT HERE.

---

september 7

WHAT ARE YOU CURRENTLY MOST PROUD OF ABOUT YOURSELF?

september 8

HOW ARE YOU ASSURING YOURSELF THAT YOU ARE ENOUGH?

_____

_____

_____

_____

_____

_____

_____

_____

september 9

WHAT WOULD YOU DO DIFFERENTLY IF YOU KNEW YOU WOULD NEVER BE JUDGED?

september 10

WHAT IS SOMETHING THAT IS REOCCURRING IN YOUR SUBCONSCIOUS?

september 11

COMPARISON IS THE THIEF OF JOY. HOW HAVE YOU COMPARED YOURSELF TO OTHERS IN THE PAST?

september 12

WHAT WAS THE NICEST THING YOU'VE DONE FOR YOURSELF RECENTLY?

_____

_____

_____

_____

_____

_____

_____

_____

september 13

WE SHED LAYERS OF OURSELVES AS WE GROW. WHAT LAYER ARE YOU CURRENTLY SHEDDING?

_____
_____
_____
_____
_____
_____
_____
_____

september 14

WHAT DYSFUNCTION HAVE YOU NORMALIZED UNINTENTIONALLY?

_____
_____
_____
_____
_____
_____
_____
_____

september 15

WHAT ARE SOME OF YOUR STRENGTHS?

_____
_____
_____
_____
_____
_____
_____
_____
_____

september 16

WHO GAVE YOU RECENTLY FORGAVE AND WHY?

_____
_____
_____
_____
_____
_____
_____
_____
_____

september 17

WHAT HAS BEEN YOUR GREATEST ACCOMPLISHMENT THIS FAR IN LIFE?

_____
_____
_____
_____
_____
_____
_____
_____

september 18

LETTING GO IS HARD TO DO. WHAT IS SOMETHING THAT YOU NEED TO RELEASE? RELEASE IT NOW.

september 19

WHAT IS SOMETHING THAT YOU WANT TO WORK TOWARDS HEALING SOON?

_____
_____
_____
_____
_____
_____
_____
_____

september 20

FEAR IS A LEARNED EMOTION WE MUST LEARN TO LET GO OF. WHAT ARE YOU MOST FEARFUL OF? RELEASE THAT ENERGY OF FEAR.

_____

_____

_____

_____

_____

_____

_____

_____

september 21

WHAT IS ONE TRAIT THAT YOU HAVE LEARNED TO LOVE AND WHY?

_____
_____
_____
_____
_____
_____
_____
_____

september 22

HOW HAVE YOU REINVENTED YOURSELF?

_____

_____

_____

_____

_____

_____

_____

_____

september 23

HAVE YOU EVER BEEN TOXIC TO SOMONE? HOW DID YOU RECONCILE THAT?

september 24

WHO HAVE YOU NOT BECOME YET?

_____

_____

_____

_____

_____

_____

_____

_____

_____

september 25

HOW ARE YOU SHOWING GRATITUDE FOR THE DIRECTION YOUR LIFE IS TAKING?

_____
_____
_____
_____
_____
_____
_____
_____

september 26

HOW ARE YOU ACTIVELY WORKING TO BETTER YOURSELF MENTALLY?

_____

_____

_____

_____

_____

_____

_____

_____

september 27

WHAT HAS FED YOUR SOUL LATELY?

september 28

I WHOLE HEARTEDLY BELIEVE.....

---

september 29

THERE ARE MOMENTS IN TIME THAT WILL ALTER THE COURSE OF YOUR LIFE. DESCRIBE A LIFE CHANGING MOMENT.

_____
_____
_____
_____
_____
_____
_____
_____

september 30

october 1

OCTOBER AFFIRMATIONS.

october 2

WHAT'S A MEMORY THAT MAKES YOU SMILE? HOW OFTEN DO YOU REVISIT THIS?

_____
_____
_____
_____
_____
_____
_____
_____
_____

october 3

IT'S OK TO NOT BE OK. HOW DO YOU KEEP YOURSELF POSITIVE IN MOMENTS YOU MAY BE NOT FEEL YOUR BEST?

_____

_____

_____

_____

_____

_____

_____

_____

october 4

TIME IS OF THE ESSENCE. WHAT HAVE YOU PUT OFF THAT YOU NEED TO COMPLETE?

october 5

HOW HAS SOCIETY CHANGED YOU?GRO

october 6

WHEN WAS THE LAST TIME YOU ENJOYED YOURSELF IN A GROUP SETTING?

_____

_____

_____

_____

_____

_____

_____

_____

october 7

I AM NO LONGER UPSET ABOUT

_____

_____

_____

_____

_____

_____

_____

_____

october 8

WHAT ARE SOME CHARACTER FLAWS THAT YOU WOULD LIKE TO CHANGE ABOUT YOURSELF?

october 9

YOUR CIRCUMSTANCES NOW WILL BE YOUR TESTIMONY LATER. HOW DOES IT START?

october 10

WHAT ARE TRAITS THAT MAKE YOU FEEL SPECIAL?

_____

_____

_____

_____

_____

_____

_____

_____

october 11

NAME A TIME WHEN PRIDE GOT IN THE WAY OF YOUR BETTER JUDGEMENT.

october 12

ocotber 13

october 14

ocotber 15

ocotber 16

ocotber 17

october 18

THINK OF YOUR BIGGEST GOAL AND WRITE THE STEPS YOU NEED TO TAKE TO GET THERE.

_____

_____

_____

_____

_____

_____

_____

_____

october 19

WHEN WAS THE LAST TIME YOU GOT SOMETHING OFF YOUR CHEST AND WHAT WAS IT?

_____

_____

_____

_____

_____

_____

_____

_____

october 20

IN WHAT WAYS ARE YOU STAYING IN YOUR LIGHT?

_____

_____

_____

_____

_____

_____

_____

_____

_____

october 21

WHEN WAS THE LAST TIME YOU FELT OVERWHELMED AND WHY?

_____

_____

_____

_____

_____

_____

_____

_____

_____

october 22

WHAT HAVE YOU BEEN BLAMING YOURSELF FOR THAT'S NOT YOUR FAULT?

october 23

NAME SOMETHING YOU NEEDED TO LET GO TO ELEVATE AND DESCRIBE THE PROCESS.

_____

_____

_____

_____

_____

_____

_____

_____

october 24

YOUR DIET IS NOT JUST FOOD BUT ALL THE THINGS YOU TAKE IN. WHAT HAVE YOU BEEN CONSUMING?

october 25

WHAT DOES YOUR DARKEST MOMENTS LOOK LIKE?

_____

_____

_____

_____

_____

_____

_____

_____

_____

october 26

WHAT DOES YOUR DREAM HOME LOOK LIKE?

october 27

LAUGHTER IS GOOD FOR THE SPIRIT. WHEN WAS THE LAST TIME YOU HAD A GOOD LAUGH?

october 28

WHAT WAYS HAVE YOU BEEN ADVENTUROUS LATELY?

_____
_____
_____
_____
_____
_____
_____
_____
_____

social media is a huge part of our diet. follow and unfollow as needed.

october 29

IN WHAT WAYS HAVE YOU BEEN PUTTING YOURSELF FIRST?

_____
_____
_____
_____
_____
_____
_____
_____
_____

october 30

WHAT ARE YOUR HOBBIES AND HAVE YOU BEEN INVESTING TIME INTO THEM?

_____
_____
_____
_____
_____
_____
_____
_____
_____

october 31

TIME TO REFLECT ON THIS MONTH.
(FEELINGS, ACCOMPLISHMENTS, ETC.)

_____
_____
_____
_____
_____
_____
_____
_____
_____

november 1

NOVEMBER AFFIRMATIONS.

_____

_____

_____

_____

_____

_____

_____

_____

_____

november 2

CHANGE IS CONSTANT, HOW ARE YOU CURRENTLY CHANGING?

_____

_____

_____

_____

_____

_____

_____

_____

november 3

WHAT ASSURANCE DO YOU HAVE KNOWING THAT YOUR MENTAL HEALTH IS IN GOOD CONDITION?

november 4

NAME THREE SMALL GOALS FOR THE MONTH.

_____
_____
_____
_____
_____
_____
_____
_____

november 5

GROWTH IS NOT ALWAYS NOTICEABLE TO THOSE AROUND US. REMIND YOURSELF OF THE GROWTH YOU'VE MADE.

_____

_____

_____

_____

_____

_____

_____

_____

november 6

WRITE DOWN 3 LONG TERM GOALS AND WAYS TO FOLLOW THROUGH.

_____

_____

_____

_____

_____

_____

_____

_____

november 7

TODAY I'M NOT GOING TO.....

_____

_____

_____

_____

_____

_____

_____

_____

_____

november 8

WHAT WAS THE MOST VALUABLE LESSON YOU'VE LEARNED THIS PAST YEAR?

_____
_____
_____
_____
_____
_____
_____
_____
_____

november 9

HOW ARE YOU ENCOURAGING TO OTHERS?

november 10

HOW ARE YOU DOING THINGS DIFFERENTLY FROM YOUR PARENTS/GUARDIANS?

_____
_____
_____
_____
_____
_____
_____
_____

november 11

HOW HAVE YOU LOST YOURSELF IN SOMEONE OR SOMETHING?

_____
_____
_____
_____
_____
_____
_____
_____
_____

november 12

WHAT DID YOU LEARN FROM YOUR CURRENT/LAST RELATIONSHIP?

_____
_____
_____
_____
_____
_____
_____
_____
_____

november 13

IF YOU COULD GO BACK IN TIME FOR A MOMENT, WHAT ERA WOULD YOU VISIT AND WHY?

november 14

IN WHAT WAYS ARE YOU FINISHING THIS YEAR STRONG?

_____

_____

_____

_____

_____

_____

_____

_____

november 15

FAVORITE QUOTE?

---

november 16

WHAT ARE SOME THINGS THAT YOU THOUGHT YOU COULDN'T LIVE WITHOUT, THAT YOU DID NOT NEED?

_____
_____
_____
_____
_____
_____
_____
_____

november 17

WHEN EXPERIENCING DARK TIMES, HOW DO YOU PULL YOURSELF CLOSER TO YOUR LIGHT?

_____

_____

_____

_____

_____

_____

_____

_____

_____

november 18

IMAGINE YOURSELF IN A PLACE WITHOUT FEAR, DOUBT AND STRESS. WHAT IS THIS PLACE?

november 19

WHAT ARE YOUR FAVORITE THINGS TO DO WITH YOUR ME TIME?

_____
_____
_____
_____
_____
_____
_____
_____

november 20

VENT HERE.

_____

_____

_____

_____

_____

_____

_____

_____

_____

november 21

AS I MATURE, I REALIZE.....

_____

_____

_____

_____

_____

_____

_____

_____

november 22

ANY ROOM FOR NEW FRIENDS? WHY OR WHY NOT?

_____

_____

_____

_____

_____

_____

_____

_____

_____

november 23

WHAT IS THE LATEST PROJECT YOU'RE WORKING ON AND HOW IS IT COMING ALONG?

november 24

WHAT ARE SOME THINGS YOU USED TO CARE ABOUT 10 YEARS AGO THAT YOU'VE OVERCOME?

_____

_____

_____

_____

_____

_____

_____

_____

november 25

WHO DO YOU FEEL YOU SHOULD MAKE AMENDS WITH AND WHY?

_____

_____

_____

_____

_____

_____

_____

_____

we experience trauma, we are not defined by it.

november 26

WHAT ARE YOUR CURRENT SELF-CARE PRACTICES?

_____

_____

_____

_____

_____

_____

_____

_____

november 27

NAME THE LITTLE THINGS YOU'RE CURRENTLY GRATEFUL FOR?

_____

_____

_____

_____

_____

_____

_____

_____

november 28

HOW ARE YOU CURRENTLY DOING THE INNER WORK OF HEALING?

_____
_____
_____
_____
_____
_____
_____
_____
_____

november 29

THE LAST TIME YOU GAVE SOMEONE YOUR HEART, WHAT HAPPENED?

_____

_____

_____

_____

_____

_____

_____

_____

november 30

HOW DID YOU HANDLE YOUR EMOTIONS THE LAST TIME YOU WERE UPSET?

_____

_____

_____

_____

_____

_____

_____

_____

november 31

TIME TO REFLECT ON THIS MONTH. (FEELINGS, ACCOMPLISHMENTS, ETC.)

_____
_____
_____
_____
_____
_____
_____
_____
_____

december 1

DECEMEBER AFFIRMATIONS.

_____
_____
_____
_____
_____
_____
_____
_____

december 2

A CLEAR SPACE, A CLEAR MIND. WHAT ARE SOME BELONGINGS YOU COULD DONATE?

_____

_____

_____

_____

_____

_____

_____

_____

december 3

WHAT BATTLE ARE YOU CURRENTLY GOING THROUGH AND HOW WILL YOU OVERCOME IT?

_____

_____

_____

_____

_____

_____

_____

_____

december 4

IN A YEAR'S TIME, WHAT ARE SOME CHANGES THAT YOU WOULD LIKE TO MAKE PHYSICALLY?

december 5

IF YOU COULD DO SOMETHING SPECIAL TO PROGRESS YOUR HOMETOWN, WHAT WOULD IT BE?

december 6

WHAT ARE SOME THINGS YOU ABSOLUTELY CANNOT LIVE WITHOUT?

_____
_____
_____
_____
_____
_____
_____
_____
_____

december 7

WHAT ARE SOME THINGS YOU DISLIFE ABOUT YOURSELF?

_____
_____
_____
_____
_____
_____
_____
_____

december 8

WHO'S YOUR FAVORITE PERSON YOU LIKE TO VENT TO AND WHY?

_____

_____

_____

_____

_____

_____

_____

_____

december 9

IF YOU COULD, WHAT WOULD YOU CHANGE ABOUT SOCIETY?

december 10

REFLECT ON THE LAST 3 MONTHS. WHAT IS SOMETHING THAT YOU REGRET LETTING GET TO YOU?

_____
_____
_____
_____
_____
_____
_____
_____
_____

december 11

YESTERDAY I FELT _____ TODAY I FEEL _____ TOMORROW I WANT TO FEEL _____.

december 12

WHAT WAS THE LONGEST PERIOD OF TIME YOU'VE BEEN SINGLE AND WHAT DID YOU LEARN DURING THAT PERIOD?

_____

_____

_____

_____

_____

_____

_____

_____

december 13

IN WHAT WAYS DO YOU KEEP YOUR FAITH STRONG?

_____

_____

_____

_____

_____

_____

_____

_____

december 14

WHAT'S THE MOST THOUGHTFUL THING YOU'VE EVER DONE FOR SOMEONE?

_____
_____
_____
_____
_____
_____
_____
_____

december 15

IF YOU COULD DO ANYTHING OVER AGAIN, WHAT WOULD IT BE?

_____

_____

_____

_____

_____

_____

_____

_____

december 16

WORK SMART, NOT HARD. HOW ARE YOU WORKING SMART TOWARDS YOUR GOALS?

_____
_____
_____
_____
_____
_____
_____
_____
_____

december 17

HOW ARE YOU MAKING SURE YOU GET A COMPLETE NUTRITIONAL DIET?

december 18

WHAT NO LONGER SERVES YOUR PURPOSE?

_____
_____
_____
_____
_____
_____
_____
_____
_____

december 19

WHAT MINDSET ARE YOU CURRENTLY DETACHING FROM?

_____

_____

_____

_____

_____

_____

_____

_____

_____

december 20

WE ALL HAVE WANTS. WHAT ARE THE THINGS YOU NEED TO FEEL CONTENT?

_____
_____
_____
_____
_____
_____
_____
_____

december 21

WHEN WAS THE LAST TIME YOU HAD A MELTDOWN AND WHY?

_____

_____

_____

_____

_____

_____

_____

_____

december 22

WHAT WORK DO YOU FEEL LIKE YOU'RE FINALLY GETTING PAID OFF FOR?

_____
_____
_____
_____
_____
_____
_____
_____

december 23

WHEN WAS THE LAST TIME YOU UNPLUGGED FROM ALL YOUR STRESSORS?

_____

_____

_____

_____

_____

_____

_____

december 24

HOW ARE YOU FINANCIALLY INVESTING IN YOURSELF?

_____

_____

_____

_____

_____

_____

_____

_____

december 25

NAME 3 THINGS YOU'VE CUT BACK ON TO SAVE MONEY.

december 26

AT THIS VERY MOMENT, HOW DO YOU FEEL?

_____
_____
_____
_____
_____
_____
_____
_____

december 27

WHAT ARE SOME THINGS YOU RECENTLY CHANGED YOUR MIND ABOUT?

_____

_____

_____

_____

_____

_____

_____

_____

december 28

HOW ARE YOU BEING AUTHENTICALLY YOU?

_____

_____

_____

_____

_____

_____

_____

_____

december 29

HOW ARE YOU PREPARING FOR NEXT YEAR?

_____

_____

_____

_____

_____

_____

_____

_____

_____

if we do not know our history, we are inclined to repeat it

december 30

WHAT NEW HABITS ARE YOU FORMING FOR NEXT YEAR?

_____

_____

_____

_____

_____

_____

_____

_____

_____

december 31

TIME TO REFLECT ON THIS MONTH.
(FEELINGS, ACCOMPLISHMENTS, ETC.)

_____

_____

_____

_____

_____

_____

_____

_____

FOR MORE PLEASE VISIT:
XOASHACO.COM

Made in the USA
Coppell, TX
07 January 2021